The Little Girl

Who Wasn't Tired

by

Kathy Grace

and

Marlon Grace

ISBN:1979301921
ISBN-13: 978-1979301923

This book

is dedicated to

my granddaughter,

my heart-cakes,

My Nola bean.

There once was a little girl who was never tired.

Whenever her mom tried
to put her down for a nap,
or to sleep for the night,
she would cry and
complain and put up a fight!

3

"I don't want to take a nap!
I don't want to go to bed!
I don't want to do those things!
I'm not tired," she said.

She did what she loved
with crafts and her glue,
cutting paper with scissors
and colors of blue.

7

She hoped mom didn't notice her yawn, and send her to bed. "I'm not tired, she thought to herself, I will stay up instead!"

10

She went to a fair,
with a smile so bright and so wide,
enjoyed cookies and candy,
and a dizzying ride.

"I won't go home now!
I won't go home ever!
I'm not going to bed, for I... will be clever!"

She flipped and she split,
and stood on her head,
then looked at her mom,
and looked at her bed.

16

She ignored when she saw that
her clock had said eight.
"I'm not tired.", she thought
to herself,
"The bed will just have to wait."

20

"My eyes aren't even heavy, which means I'm not tired."

"But, you must go to bed, for your time has expired."

23

"I'm not tired, I'm not tired and I won't go to sleep!"

"Then count stars on your ceiling, count dolls or count sheep!"

"When I try to count sheep, I get only to ten, and then I lose my whole place and have to start all over again!"

And so that it happened, and it
happened so late,that the sandman
indeed sealed the little girl's fate.

She was so fast asleep, and mom
was so glad, and forever so grateful,
for the day that they had.

28

29

"My sweet little girl, who's worth more than the world, shines bright like a diamond or even a pearl.
My precious little girl who is ever so sweet, little did she know, that she'd soon be fast asleep."

The End.

Acknowledgements

I would like to express my gratitude to the following people who have assisted in some way to making sure this book made it to fruition.
First my granddaughter, Nola, for being the inspiration for me writing this book.
How many times have you fussed because you did not want to go to bed?
And how many times didn't you believe gammy when I would tell you that one day you would be happy to take a nap or go to bed, because sleep is a reward where you can dream and put everything to rest?

Next, I would like to thank
my first born, Marlon, for
always being so eager to
"help moms out" when
I would have a writer's block.
You would so effortlessly
take my words and ideas
and string them into
lyrical and poetical flows.

To my daughter, Marlo,
my other genetic masterpiece,
for contributing your
keen sense of design
perfection and making
for certain that
everything was just right.

To my son Rodney and his
wonderful wife Lourdes for
dealing with me going back
and forth just trying to
find the right little
girl illustration to
use for the book.

Also, I'd like to thank my niece
Tanna for always being
available when
aunty needed to talk.

Last but not least, thanks
to my bestie Patti
for being so eloquent
with her one liners.
And also for demonstrating
patience and willingness
while contributing to my vision.

Authors
Kathy Grace and
Marlon Grace

Illustrator
Seerat Fatima

Contributing Illustrator
Nola Grace

Designer
Marlo Grace

Editor
Marlon Grace

contact
envydas@aol.com

Made in the USA
San Bernardino, CA
23 January 2018